SOUNDS OF LANGUAGE READERS

Sounds
of Laughter

by Bill Martin, Jr.

Linguistic Adviser, W. Cabell Greet

CALIFORNIA STATE SERIES
Published by
CALIFORNIA STATE DEPARTMENT OF EDUCATION
Sacramento, 1969

Acknowledgments

The following selections are adapted from Little Owl Books copyright © 1963 by Holt, Rinehart and Winston, Inc., except as noted.

"Good Night," picture, from MY LITTLE BROTHER.

"The Old Woman and her Pig," from THE OLD WOMAN AND HER PIG.

"The Three Billy-Goats Gruff," from THE THREE BILLY-GOATS GRUFF.

"Keep a Poem in Your Pocket," picture, from THE SUN IS A STAR. Poem, "Keep a Poem in Your Pocket" by Beatrice Schenk de Regniers, from SOMETHING SPECIAL copyright © 1958 by Beatrice Schenck de Regniers and reprinted by permission of the publishers, Harcourt, Brace and World, Inc. and William Collins & Sons, Ltd.

The following selections are adapted from Young Owl Books copyright © 1964 by Holt, Rinehart and Winston, Inc., except as noted.

"The Funny Old Man and the Funny Old Woman," from THE FUNNY OLD MAN AND THE FUNNY OLD WOMAN by Martha Barber.

"Here's a Picture for Storytelling," (page 36) from BICYCLE SONGS OF SAFETY by Jill and Lawrence Grossman.

"A Maker of Boxes," from A MAKER OF BOXES by H. R. Wittram.

"Here's a Picture for Storytelling" (page 92); "Nine Little Goblins," from ELEVEN AND THREE ARE POETRY compiled by Sally Nohelty. Poem, "Nine Little Goblins," from JOYFUL POEMS FOR CHILDREN by James Whitcomb Riley copyright © 1941, 1946, 1960 by Lesley Payne, Elizabeth Eitel Meisse and Edmund H. Eitel and reprinted by permission.

"Old Lucy Lindy and the Pies," from OLD LUCY LINDY by Leland Jacobs.

"Joey Kangaroo," from JOEY KANGAROO by Patricia K. Miller and Iran L. Seligman.

"Little Red-Cap," from LITTLE RED-CAP by the Brothers Grimm, translated by Werner Linz.

"Here's a Picture for Storytelling," (page 144) from WHEN CHRISTMAS COMES by Doris Whitman.

"Growing Up, Growing Older," from GROWING UP, GROWING OLDER by the North Shore Senior Center.

"The River Is a Piece of Sky," from POETRY FOR YOUNG SCIENTISTS compiled by Leland B. Jacobs and Sally Nohelty. Poem, "The River Is a Piece of Sky," from THE REASON FOR THE PELICAN by John Ciardi copyright © 1959 by John Ciardi and reprinted by permission of the publishers, J. B. Lippincott Company.

"Knots on a Counting Rope," from KNOTS ON A COUNTING ROPE by Bill Martin, Jr., pictures by Joe Smith.

Contents

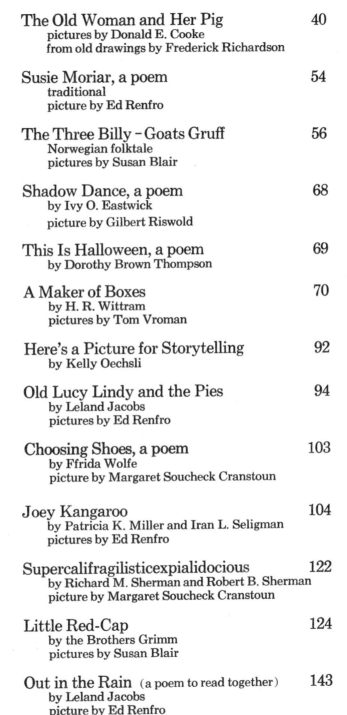

Sounds of Laughter

picture by Ed Renfro

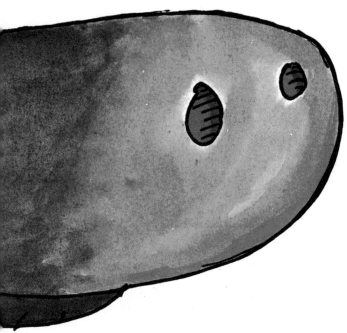

Listen, Listen

Listen, listen and you shall hear
How the old cow died with a bug in her ear.
The bug flew out,
The wind blew in,
The old cow's up and gone again.

from Ray Wood's
collection of American folklore

The Funny Old Man

by Martha Barber,

A funny old man and a funny old woman
   sat by the fire one night.
"Funny old man," old woman said,
   "I don't know what to do.
When I went to the barn to milk the cow,
   the funny old cow wouldn't moo."

and the Funny Old Woman

pictures by Ed Renfro

The funny old man scratched his head.
"I know what to do," he said.
"Take her to town to see Doctor Brown,
    and bring her home in the morning.
    That's what you do when the cow won't moo."

"But she's out in the woodshed lying down.
How will you take the cow to town
    and bring her back in the morning?"

"If she can't walk," said the funny old man,
    "I'll push her in the wheelbarrow if I can,
    and walk her home in the morning."

"But the goat's asleep in the wheelbarrow.
Where shall I put the goat?"

"Put the goat on top of the garden gate.
  The goat can sleep there very late
    till the cow comes home in the morning."

"But the rooster is roosting on the garden gate.
  Where shall I put the rooster?"

"Put the rooster in the butter churn,
    so tight that he can't twist or turn
    till the cow comes home in the morning."

"But my nice fresh butter is in the churn.
    Where shall I put the butter?"

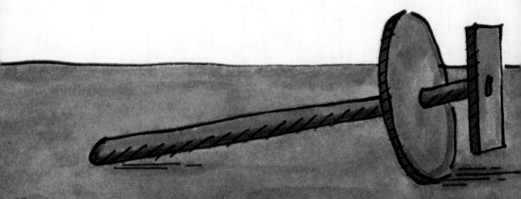

"Put the butter on a string in the garden pool,
  and it will keep there fresh and cool
  till the cow comes home in the morning."

"But the fish is in the garden pool.
 Where shall I put the fish?"

"Put the fish in some water in the old washtub,
  so he can give his fins a scrub
  till the cow comes home in the morning."

"But the cat's asleep in the old washtub.
 Where shall I put the cat?"

"Put the cat in the fruit bowl. Then she'll dream
of nice red strawberries laced with cream
till the cow comes home in the morning."

"But the figs are in the fruit bowl.
Where shall I put the figs?"

"Put the figs in the barn on a pile of wheat.
They'll keep quite firm and fresh and sweet
till the cow comes home in the morning."

"But the pig is sleeping on the pile of wheat.
What shall I do with the pig?"

"Put the pig on a pillow in the feather bed,
to snooze and snore," the old man said,
"till the cow comes home in the morning."

"No," said the woman. "I sleep on the bed.
Where shall I lay my funny old head?"

The old man cried, "Put the pig in the bed!
And you can stand on your funny old head
     till the cow comes home in the morning."

So the funny old woman flipped up on her head.
"It's really quite cozy here," she said,
     "till the cow comes home in the morning."

Then late that night the funny old man
pushed the funny old cow to town.

They rolled in the light of the bright, full moon
till they found old Doctor Brown.

The doctor thumped on the old cow's hide,
he tickled her tonsils and looked inside.
"Old man," said the doctor, "your cow's not sick.
She merely wanted the ride!"

The old man cried, "Can this be true?"
The cow replied with a happy "Moo."

And they both went home in the morning.

Here's a Picture for Storytelling

by Herbert McClure

The Critic

by John Farrar

Sometimes when it is bedtime,
My mother comes to me,
She takes me from my warm bed,
And sits me on her knee.

And it is very pleasant
To hear her golden voice,
Reading bedtime stories
According to my choice.

And when she reads me poems,
The kind that I like best—
The music of them lulls me
Quite gently to my rest.

Now, often when I'm wakeful
I count a million sheep—
But poems are far, far better
For putting boys to sleep.

picture by Carole Kofod Butterfield

Good Night

by Thomas Hood

Here's a body—there's a bed!
There's a pillow—here's a head!
There's a curtain—here's a light!
There's a puff—and so good night!

The Old Woman and Her Pig

pictures adapted by Donald E. Cooke,
from old drawings by Frederick Richardson

An Old Woman found a sixpence.
She said,
"What shall I do with this sixpence?
I will buy a pig."

So she bought a pig.

On the way home they came to a stile.

The Old Woman said,

   "Pig, pig, jump over the stile."

The pig said,

   "I will not jump over the stile."

The Old Woman went on
    till she met a dog.
She said,
    "Dog, dog, bite pig!
    Pig will not jump over the stile,
    and I shall not get home to-night."
The dog said,
    "No, I will not bite pig."

The Old Woman went on
   till she met a stick.
She said,
   "Stick, stick, beat dog!
   Dog will not bite pig.
   Pig will not jump over the stile,
   and I shall not get home to-night."
The stick said,
   "No, I will not beat dog."

F.R.

The Old Woman went on
    till she met a fire.
She said,
    "Fire, fire, burn stick!
    Stick will not beat dog.
    Dog will not bite pig.
    Pig will not jump over the stile,
    and I shall not get home to-night."
The fire said,
    "No, I will not burn stick."

The Old Woman went on
   till she met some water.
She said,
   "Water, water, quench fire!
   Fire will not burn stick.
   Stick will not beat dog.
   Dog will not bite pig.
   Pig will not jump over the stile,
   and I shall not get home to-night."
The water said,
   "No, I will not quench fire."

The Old Woman went on
    till she met an ox.
She said,
    "Ox, ox, drink water!
    Water will not quench fire.
    Fire will not burn stick.
    Stick will not beat dog.
    Dog will not bite pig.
    Pig will not jump over the stile,
    and I shall not get home to-night."
The ox said,
    "No, I will not drink water."

The Old Woman went on
  till she met a butcher.
She said,
  "Butcher, butcher, kill ox!
  Ox will not drink water.
  Water will not quench fire.
  Fire will not burn stick.
  Stick will not beat dog.
  Dog will not bite pig.
  Pig will not jump over the stile,
  and I shall not get home to-night."
The butcher said,
  "No, I will not kill ox."

The Old Woman went on
 till she met a rope.
She said,
 "Rope, rope, hang butcher!
 Butcher will not kill ox.
 Ox will not drink water.
 Water will not quench fire.
 Fire will not burn stick.
 Stick will not beat dog.
 Dog will not bite pig.
 Pig will not jump over the stile,
 and I shall not get home to-night."
The rope said,
 "No, I will not hang butcher."

The Old Woman went on
   till she met a rat.
She said, "Rat, rat, gnaw rope!
   Rope will not hang butcher.
   Butcher will not kill ox.
   Ox will not drink water.
   Water will not quench fire.
   Fire will not burn stick.
   Stick will not beat dog.
   Dog will not bite pig.
   Pig will not jump over the stile,
   and I shall not get home to-night."
The rat said, "Get me some cheese.
   Then I will gnaw the rope."

The Old Woman got some cheese.

She gave it to the rat.

Then the rat

began to gnaw the rope.

The rope began

to hang the butcher.

The butcher began

to kill the ox.

The ox began to drink the water.

The water began to quench the fire.

The fire began to burn the stick.

The stick began to beat the dog.

The dog began to bite the pig.

The pig jumped over the stile,
and the Old Woman
got home that night.

Susie Moriar

traditional,
picture by Ed Renfro

This is the story
Of Susie Moriar.
It started one night
As she sat by the fire.

The fire was so hot,
Susie jumped in a pot.
The pot was so black,
Susie dropped in a crack.

The crack was so narrow,
Susie climbed on a wheelbarrow.
The wheelbarrow was so low,
Susie fell in the snow.

The snow was so white,
Susie stayed there all night.
The night was so long,
Susie sang a song.

The song was so sweet,
Susie ran down the street. The street was so clean, Susie picked up a bean.

The bean was so hard, Susie dropped it in lard. The lard was so greasy, Susie nearly jumped fleecy.

And when she came down,
She ran through the town.
The town was so big,
Susie jumped on a pig.
The pig jumped so high,
He touched the sky—
He touched the sky
And he couldn't jump higher,

But, oh, what, a ride had Susie Moriar.

The Three Billy-Goats Gruff

A Norwegian folktale,
woodcuts by Susan Blair

Once on a time there were three billy-goats,
    who were to go up to the hillside
    to make themselves fat,
    and the name of all three was "Gruff."

On the way up was a bridge;
    and under the bridge lived a great ugly Troll,
    with eyes as big as saucers,
    and a nose as long as a poker.

So first of all
came the youngest billy-goat Gruff
to cross the bridge.

"*Trip, trap! trip, trap!*" went the bridge.
"WHO'S THAT tripping over my bridge?"
roared the Troll.

"Oh! it is only I,
    the tiniest billy-goat Gruff;
    and I'm going up to the hillside
    to make myself fat,"
    said the billy-goat.

"Now, I'm coming to gobble you up,"
  said the Troll.
"Oh no! pray don't take me.
  I'm too little, that I am," said the billy-goat;
  "wait a bit
  till the second billy-goat Gruff comes,
  he's much bigger."

"Well, be off with you!" said the Troll.

A little while after
   came the second billy-goat Gruff
   to cross the bridge.
"Trip, Trap! Trip, Trap! Trip, Trap!"
   went the bridge.

"WHO'S THAT tripping over my bridge?"
   roared the Troll.

"Oh! it's the second billy-goat Gruff,
   and I'm going up to the hillside
   to make myself fat,"
   said the billy-goat,
   who hadn't such a small voice.

"Now, I'm coming to gobble you up,"
    said the Troll.

"Oh, no! don't take me;
    wait a little till the big billy-goat Gruff comes,
    he's much bigger,"

"Very well, be off with you!"
    said the Troll.

But just then up came the big billy-goat Gruff.

"TRIP, TRAP! TRIP, TRAP!

went the bridge, for the billy-goat was so heavy

that the bridge creaked and groaned under him.

"WHO'S THAT tripping over my bridge?"

roared the Troll.

"IT'S I! THE BIG BILLY-GOAT GRUFF,"

said the billy-goat

who had an ugly hoarse voice of his own.

"Now, I'm coming to gobble you up,"

roared the Troll.

"Well, come along! I've got two spears,
   And I'll poke your eyeballs out at your ears;
   I've got besides two curling-stones,
   And I'll crush you to bits, body and bones."

That was what the big billy-goat said;
   and so he flew at the Troll
   and poked his eyes out with his horns, and
   crushed him to bits, body and bones,
   and tossed him out into the burn,
   and after that he went up to the hillside.

There the billy-goats got so fat
    they were scarce able to walk home again;
    and if the fat hasn't fallen off them,
    why, they're still fat; and so:

Snip,
    snap,
        snout,
            This tale's told out.

Shadow Dance

O Shadow,
Dear Shadow,
Come, Shadow,
And dance!
On the wall
In the firelight
Let both of
Us prance!
I raise my
Arms, thus!
And you raise
Your arms, so!
And dancing
And leaping
And laughing
We go!
From the wall
To the ceiling
From ceiling
To wall,
Just you and
I, Shadow,
And none else
At all.
      by Ivy O. Eastwick

This Is Halloween

Goblins on the doorstep,
  Phantoms in the air,
Owls on witches' gateposts
  Giving stare for stare,
Cats on flying broomsticks,
  Bats against the moon,
Stirrings round of fate-cakes
  With a solemn spoon,
Whirling apple parings,
  Figures draped in sheets
Dodging, disappearing,
  Up and down the streets,
Jack-o'-lanterns grinning,
  Shadows on a screen,
Shrieks and starts and laughter —
  This is Halloween!

by Dorothy Brown Thompson

picture by Gilbert Riswold

69

A Maker of Boxes

by H. R. Wright,
pictures by Tom Vroman

Hello! My name is Albert.

I'm a maker of boxes.

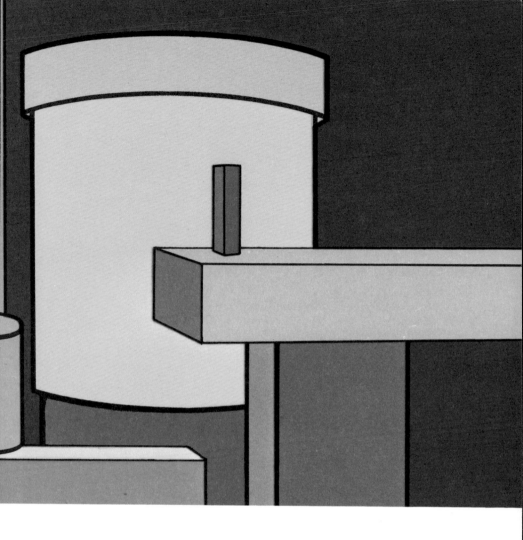

I make paper boxes,
and cardboard boxes,
and wooden boxes,

and square boxes,
and round boxes,
and long boxes,
and short boxes,
and little boxes,
and big boxes,

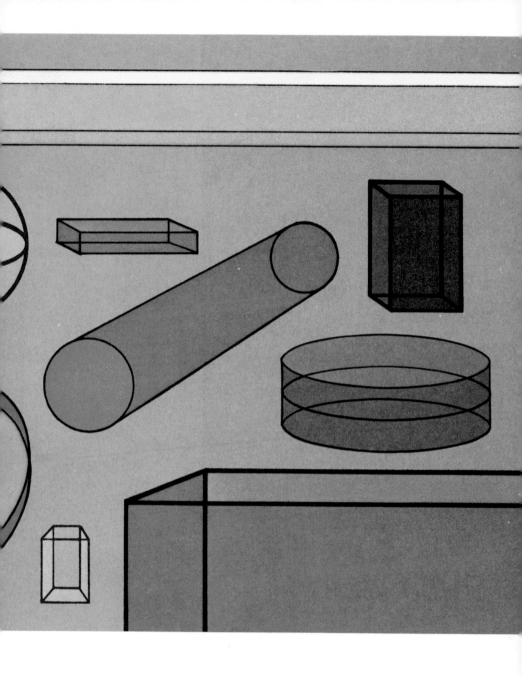

..... and all of them are empty.

On Monday I make strong boxes —

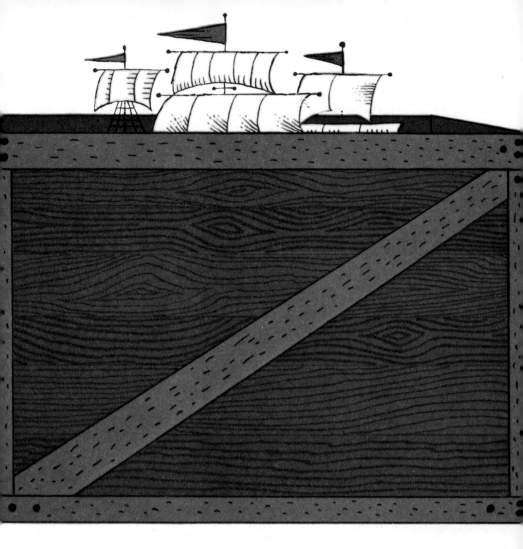

boxes for boats,
and sleds,
and bicycles,
and washing machines.

On Tuesday
I make
narrow boxes —

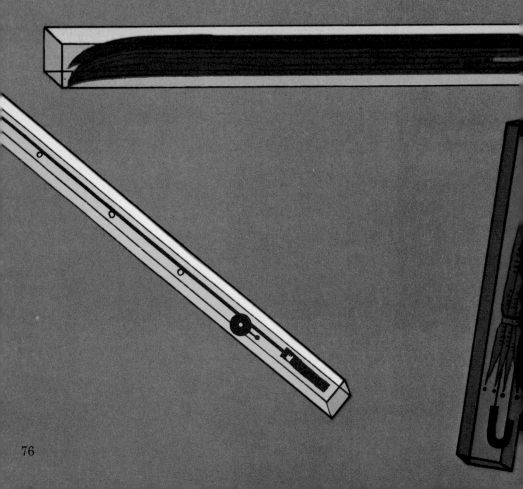

boxes for picture frames,
and skis,
and umbrellas,
and fishing poles,
and ant houses.

On Wednesday
I make cozy boxes —

boxes for bird houses,
and dog houses,
and mouse houses,
and flea houses,
and tree houses,
and cookie houses.

On Thursday I make magic boxes —

boxes that walk,
and boxes that talk,
and boxes that do strange things.

On Friday I make holiday boxes —

boxes for valentines,
and fireworks,
and Halloween hats,
and Chanukah presents.

On Saturday I don't make boxes —

I draw boxes.
I draw black boxes,
and red boxes,
and blue boxes,
and green boxes,
and yellow boxes,
and orange boxes.

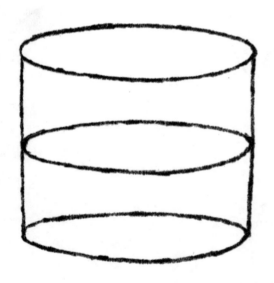

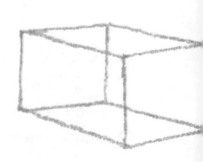

And sometimes I even draw a box
right around myself.

On April Fool's Day I make patterns
for round, fancy boxes –

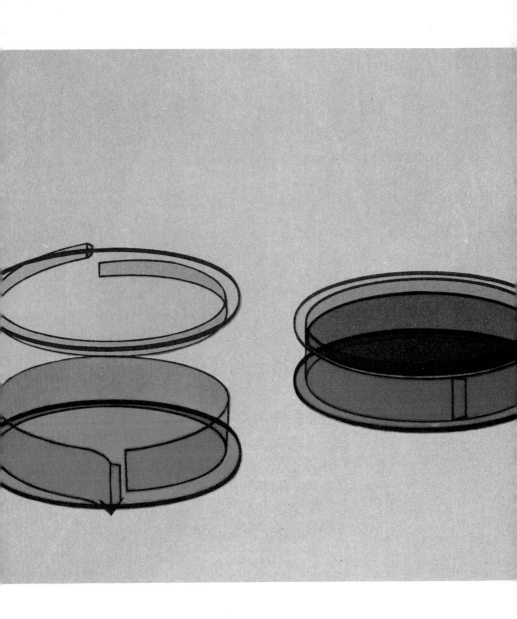

each with a bottom and a top
and long, rectangular sides.

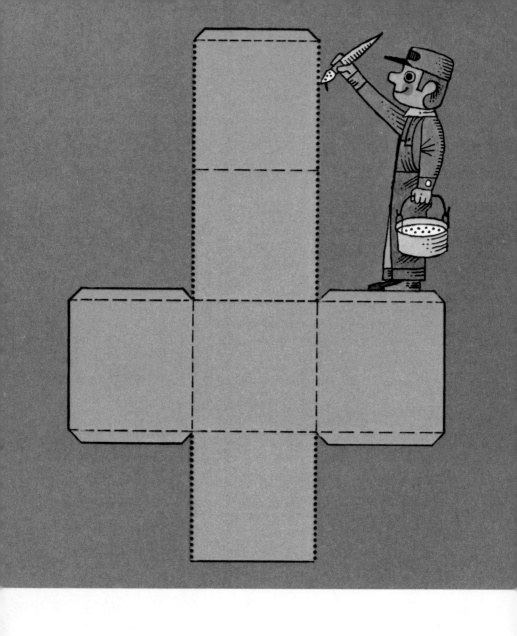

On New Year's Day
I make patterns for square, cardboard boxes –

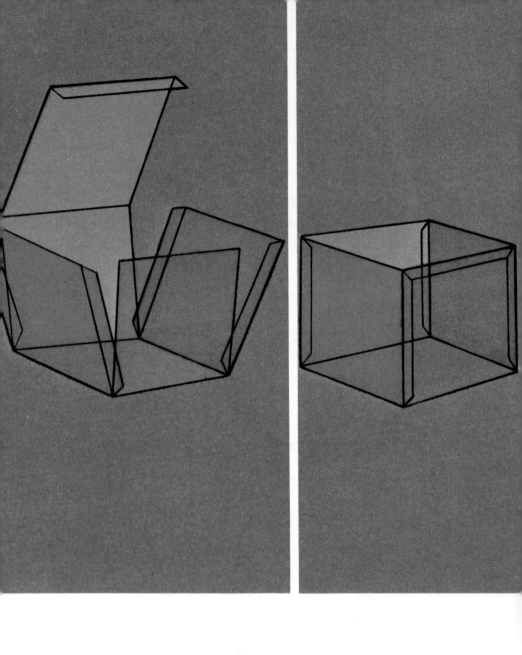

each with a bottom and a top and four sides.

On my birthday I don't make boxes.....

and I don't draw boxes.....

and I don't make patterns for boxes.....

On my birthday I go to the playground
and I play in boxes!

Here's a Picture for Storytelling

by Kelly Oechsli

Old Lucy and the Pies

by Leland Jacobs,
pictures by Ed Renfro

Old Lucy Lindy liked to bake.
She liked to bake pies.
She liked to bake cakes.

She baked many kinds of cakes:
    dark cakes,
    light cakes,
    layer cakes, and
    white cakes.

She had no trouble with her cakes.
She knew her light cakes from her
    dark cakes.
She knew her layer cakes.

Old Lucy baked many kinds of pies:
    apple pies,
    blueberry pies,
    mince pies, and
    cherry pies.

But she had trouble with her pies.
They were all covered with crust.
She could not tell one pie from another.

After it was baked, was it a mince pie?
Or was it an apple pie?

"My, what trouble!"
she said to herself.

One morning Old Lucy decided to bake.
She decided to bake five pies:

2 apple pies
1 blueberry pie
2 mince pies.

As she made the crust she had an idea.

"Now I'll know one pie from another,"
she said to herself.

She took a knife.
She put two letters in the crust.
In the mince pies she put I.M.

"That means IS MINCE,"
she said to herself.

She put two letters in the crust
of the other pies.

The letters were I.M.

"That means ISN'T MINCE,"
she said to herself.

Old Lucy baked her 2 apple pies.
She put them out on the right
     of the shelf.
She baked her 1 blueberry pie.
She put it on the right
     of the kitchen shelf.
She baked her 2 mince pies.
She put them out on the left
     of the shelf.

Old Lucy Lindy looked at her pies.
She looked left, at her mince pies.
     "I.M. means IS MINCE," she said
She looked right, at her apple
     and blueberry pies.

     "I.M.," she said, "ISN'T MINCE."
     "My, my!" she said.
     "That's a good idea! Now I know
     which pie is which."

Choosing Shoes

New shoes, new shoes,
   Red and pink and blue shoes,
Tell me, what would you choose,
   If they'd let us buy?

Buckle shoes, bow shoes,
   Pretty pointy-toe shoes,
Strappy, cappy low shoes;
   Let's have some to try.

Bright shoes, white shoes,
   Dandy-dance-by-night shoes,
Perhaps-a-little-tight shoes;
   Like some? So would I.

     But

Flat shoes, fat shoes,
   Stump-along-like-that shoes,
Wipe-them-on-the-mat shoes,
   That's the sort they'll buy.

by Ffrida Wolfe

picture by Margaret Soucheck Cranstoun

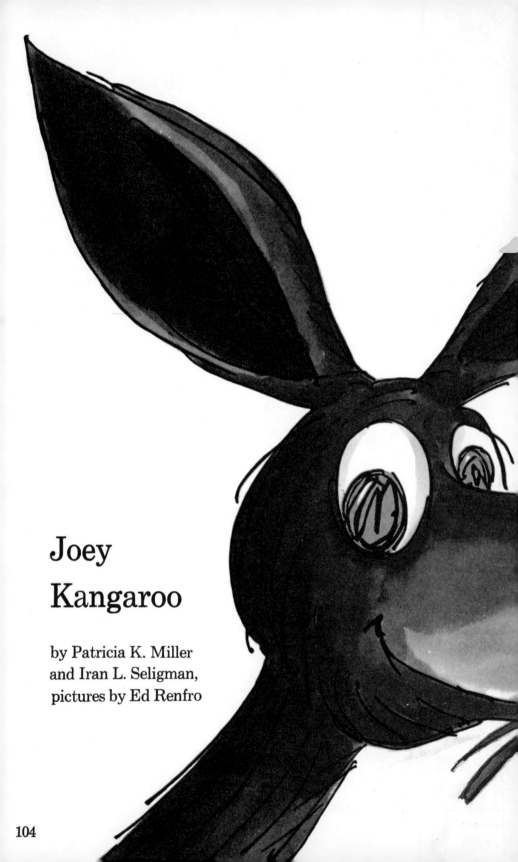

Joey
Kangaroo

by Patricia K. Miller
and Iran L. Seligman,
pictures by Ed Renfro

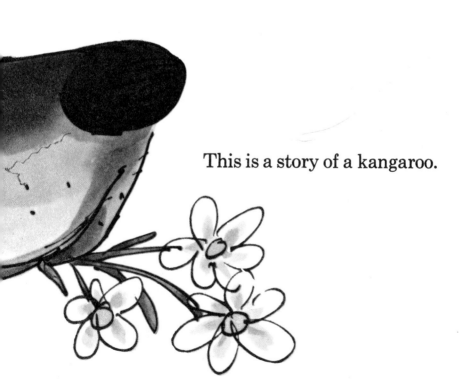

This is a story of a kangaroo.

Do you know where baby kangaroos live?
They live in their mother's "pocket." All
baby kangaroos are called joeys. The mother
kangaroo carries her joey with her, in her
pocket.

A baby kangaroo is only one inch long when it is born. It has no fur. It cannot see. As soon as it is born it crawls into the pocket.

The baby kangaroo stays in the pocket for four months. The pocket keeps it safe and warm. The mother makes milk in her body to feed the joey. If you could look in the pocket, you would see how much bigger it is growing.

In and out! In and out! Now the joey can leave the pocket. He comes out to jump and play. His mother shows him how to eat grass. Then he goes back into the pocket.

As the days go by the joey grows bigger and bigger. One day he tries to get into the pocket, but he is too big now. His mother will not let him get in.

Now the joey takes care of himself. He finds grass to eat. He jumps along with his mother.

Kangaroos live together in small groups. A group of kangaroos is called a mob. The strongest male kangaroo is the leader of the mob. He had to fight the other male kangaroos to become the leader. He had to show that he was the strongest kangaroo. He had to show that he could take care of the mob.

Kangaroos sleep during the day. At night
they move about, looking for food.

Kangaroos eat grass. They nibble leaves
from small trees. They eat fruit and vines.

Kangaroos have long, heavy tails. They rest on their tails when they sit. They push with their tails when they jump. They push down with their tails . . . and up they go! Look how high a kangaroo can jump!

Joey kangaroo is growing. One day soon he may be the leader of his mob.

Supercalifragilisticexpialidocious

Because I was afraid to speak
When I was just a lad,
Me father gave me nose a tweak
And told me I was bad.
But then one day I learned a word
That saved me achin' nose,
The biggest word you ever 'eard
And this is 'ow it goes:

Supercalifragilisticexpialidocious!
Even though the sound of it
Is something quite atrocious!
If you say it loud enough
You'll always sound precocious.
Supercalifragilisticexpialidocious!

He traveled all around the world
And ev'rywhere he went
He'd use his word and all would say,
"There goes a clever gent!"
When dukes and ma'arajas
Pass the time of day with me,
I say me spicial word and then
They ask me out to tea.

Supercalifragilisticexpialidocious!
Even though the sound of it
Is something quite atrocious!
If you say it loud enough,
You'll always sound precocious.
Supercalifragilisticexpialidocious!

by Richard M. Sherman
and Robert B. Sherman,
picture by Aliki

123

Little Red-Cap

by the Brothers Grimm,
translated by Werner Linz,
woodcuts by Susan Blair

Once upon a time there was a sweet little maiden who was loved by everyone who knew her. But her grandmother loved her most of all, and would give her anything.

One day her grandmother gave her a little cap of red velvet, which looked so pretty on her that she wore it all the time. And so she was called "Little Red-Cap."

One day her mother said to her, "Come, Little Red-Cap. Here is a piece of cake and a bottle of milk. Take these to Grandmother. She is sick and weak and they will comfort her. Now, be a good girl and remember to greet her for me. Walk carefully along the path and be sure not to go into the forest."

Little Red-Cap promised her mother that she would be careful, and that she would remember everything she had been told.

Then she started out.

Now, her grandmother lived far out in the forest, half a league from the village, and as soon as Little Red-Cap entered the forest, she met the wolf. Little Red-Cap did not know what a wicked animal he was, and so she was not afraid of him.

"Good-day, Little Red-Cap," said the wolf.

"Thank you kindly, Wolf," said Little Red-Cap.

"Where are you going so early, Little Red-Cap?"

"To Grandmother's house."

"And what are you carrying in your basket?"

"Cake and milk for Grandmother. She is sick and weak, and this will make her stronger."

"And where does your Grandmother live, Little Red-Cap?" "Another quarter of a league through the forest. Her house stands under the big oak trees. You must know where it is."

The wolf thought, "This will be a tender mouthful. Now, how do I go about getting it?"

The wolf walked along with her a little way, and then he said, "Little Red-Cap, do you not see the flowers? Do you not hear how sweetly the birds are singing? You walk along as if you were going to school back in that little village, while out here in the forest it is so gay!"

Little Red-Cap stopped and looked around. She saw how beautifully the sun's rays broke through the trees and shone on

the flowers. She thought, "Ah! If I should bring a bouquet to Grandmother, how she would like that! It is still early, and there is enough time to get there."

And she darted off into the forest to look for flowers. But as soon as she had picked one, she was sure she saw an even prettier flower just a little further on. And so she ran farther and farther from the path.

The wolf, however, went straight to Grandmother's house and knocked at the door.

"Who is outside?" asked Grandmother.

"It is Little Red-Cap," said the wolf. "I have brought you cake and milk. Open the door."

"Just lift the latch," Grandmother called. "I am too weak to get up."

The wolf lifted the latch, and the door flew open. The wolf walked in and went straight to Grandmother's bed, and then, in one gulp, he swallowed her.

Then the wolf put on her spectacles and her nightcap, climbed into the bed, and pulled the blankets up to his chin.

Little Red-Cap had been running about looking for flowers, and now she had more than she could carry. So again she set out on the path to Grandmother's house.

When she arrived, she was surprised to find the door wide open, and as she stepped into the room, she thought, "My goodness, how frightened I feel! And usually I like so much to come to Grandmother's."

She walked over to the bed and there was Grandmother in her spectacles and nightcap, looking very strange.

"Oh, Grandmother, what big ears you have," said Little Red-Cap.

"The better to hear you with, my dear."

"And Grandmother, what big eyes you have."

"The better to see you with, my dear."

"And Grandmother, what big hands you have."

"The better to hold you with, my dear."

"But Grandmother, what a dreadfully big mouth you have!"

"THE BETTER TO EAT YOU WITH, MY DEAR."

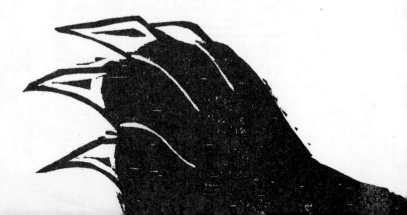

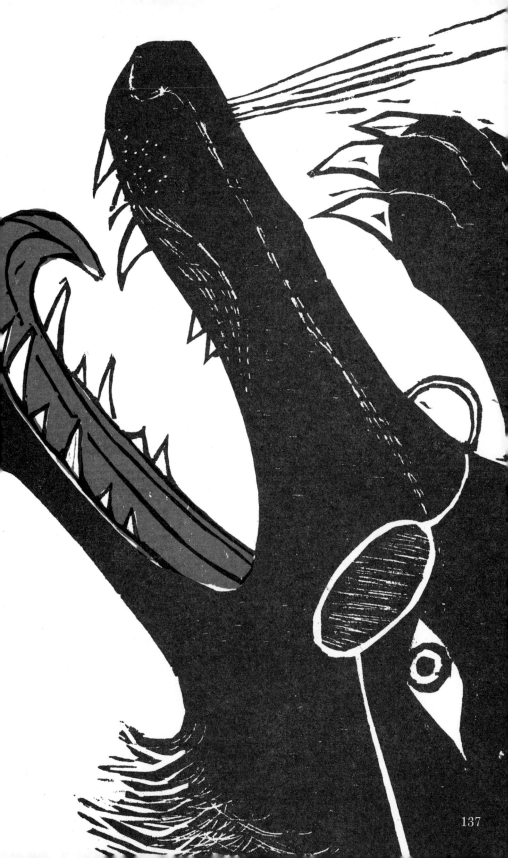

And with that, the wolf jumped up out of the bed, and swallowed poor Little Red-Cap in one gulp.

"That was a fine dinner!" said the wolf, and he climbed back into the bed.

He soon fell asleep, and began to snore very loudly.

A hunter was passing by and thought, "How that old woman can snore! I had better look in and see if she is all right."

So he went inside, and over to the bed— and there lay the wolf, the very same one that he had been hunting for so long!

The hunter was about to fire his gun. Suddenly he thought, "Surely, the wolf has swallowed the old grandmother. Perhaps she might still be saved. I shall not shoot."

So he found a pair of scissors, and began to cut open the stomach of the sleeping

wolf. He had made only a few snips, when
he saw the red cap. He cut a little more,
and out jumped the little girl.

"Oh, how frightened I was!" she cried. "How dark it was inside the wolf!"

In another moment Grandmother came out, weak and shaky. Then Little Red-Cap ran to get great, heavy rocks, with which they filled the wolf's belly. The wolf awakened and jumped up to run away, but the weight of the rocks was too much for him. He fell over backwards, and died.

And now they were very happy. The hunter took the wolf's skin and went on his way. Grandmother ate the cake and drank the milk that Little Red-Cap had brought, and soon she felt much better. And as for Little Red-Cap, she thought: "Never again, for the rest of my life, shall I leave the path and run into the forest when my mother forbids it."

Out In The Rain

Boys: Willie Duck and Wallie Duck,
Played in an April shower,
Without any rubbers on
For almost an hour.

Girls: Neither had a raincoat
And neither had a hat,
But their mother didn't worry
Or fret about that.

Boys: Of course their mother saw them,
But she didn't scold.

Girls: She didn't even tell them
That they'd both catch cold.

Boys &
Girls: Willie Duck and Wallie Duck
Were wet clear through.

Teacher: And what about their mother?

All: She was out there too!

by Leland B. Jacobs,
picture by Ed Renfro

Here's a Picture
for Storytelling

by David K. Stone

Growing Up, Growing Older
by Sonia Lisker

This is Johnny.
He is a baby.
He cannot walk.
He cannot talk.
But he can cry!
Johnny is 1 week old.

Now Johnny can walk.
He laughs and claps his hands.
He says "dada" and "mama"
and "baby."
Johnny is 1 year old.

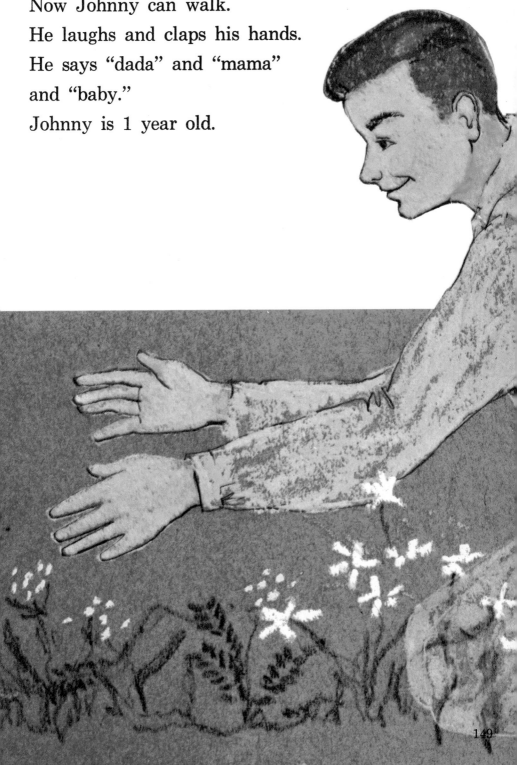

Now Johnny is 4 years old.
He is not a baby anymore.
He is a little boy.
He rides a tricycle.
and gets his hair cut
at the barber shop.
Soon he will go
to kindergarten.

Johnny is 6 years old now.
He is in the first grade.
He can skip and catch a ball.
He is learning to read.
Do you remember when you
first started to read?

Now Johnny is older. He is 8 years old.
He is in the third grade
and belongs to the Cub Scouts.
He likes to wear his uniform to school.

Now Johnny is 12.
He goes to junior high school
and plays on the football team.
He earns his own money by working
in a grocery store on Saturdays.

Johnny is still growing taller. He is 15 years old.
He delivers newspapers before school each morning.
Even if it rains and snows or the wind blows cold,
Johnny delivers his newspapers.
He is learning to work well.

John is now a young man.
He is 18 years old.
He goes to college where he is
studying to be a scientist.
Do you know anyone in college?

Now John has finished college
and has joined the Air Force.
He is known as Lt. John Miller
and he is a pilot.
He flies an airplane.

Now John is home
from the Air Force.
He is 23 years old.
He has a job at the zoo,
taking care of animals.

This is John's wedding day.

He is 27 years old.

He is marrying Peggy.

Have you ever been to a wedding?

John is now a father.
He is 35 years old.
He and Peg have two children,
Laurie and Bobby.
They come to visit him
at the zoo where he works.

Now John is 50 years old.

His picture is in the morning newspaper.

He has just been made head of the entire zoo.

John and his wife and his children
are very happy.
Have you ever seen pictures
of people you know in the paper?

Now John is 65 years old.

His picture is in the newspaper again.

He is retiring from his work at the zoo.

Now John is old.
His children have grown up,
and he is retired from his work at the zoo.
John spends many hours reading and studying
for a book he is writing
on the care and feeding of animals.
His two favorite pastimes are
working in his garden
and telling stories to his grandchildren.

Nine Little Goblins

picture by Kelly Oechsli

They all climbed up
    on a high board-fence —
Nine little goblins,
    with green-glass eyes —
Nine little goblins that had no sense,
    And couldn't tell coppers
      from cold mince-pies;
      And they all climbed up on the fence,
      and sat —
    And I asked them
      what they were staring at.

And they sang: "You're asleep!
    There is no board-fence,
    And never a goblin
      with green-glass eyes! —
'Tis only a vision the mind invents
    After a supper of cold mince-pies. —
      And you're doomed to dream this way,"
      they said, —
    "*And you sha'n't wake up*
      till you're clean plum dead!"

by James Whitcomb Riley

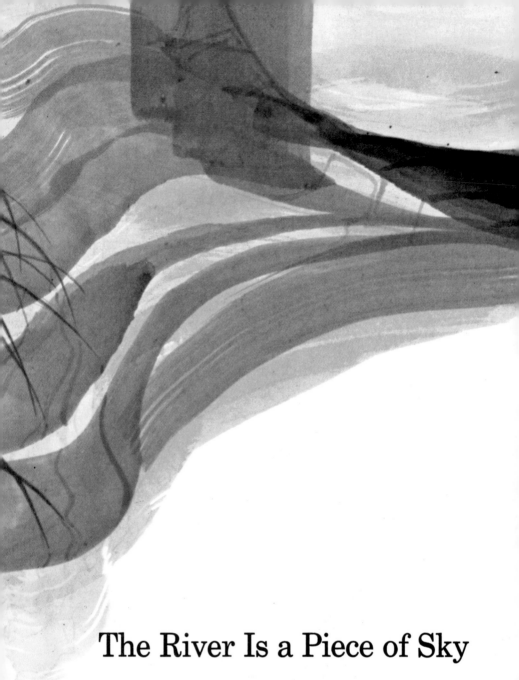

The River Is a Piece of Sky

by John Ciardi, picture by Ed Young

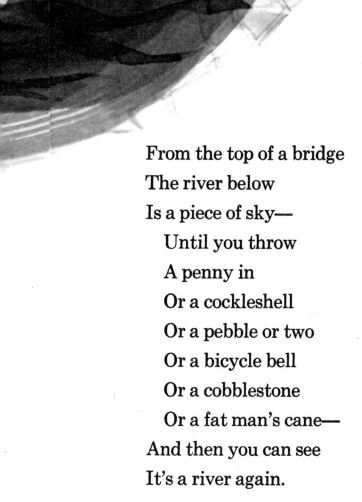

From the top of a bridge
The river below
Is a piece of sky—
　　Until you throw
　　A penny in
　　Or a cockleshell
　　Or a pebble or two
　　Or a bicycle bell
　　Or a cobblestone
　　Or a fat man's cane—
And then you can see
It's a river again.

The difference you'll see
When you drop your penny:
The river has splashes.
The sky hasn't any.

Knots on a Counting Rope

by Bill Martin, Jr.,
pictures by Joe Smith

"Grandfather, tell me the story again.
 Tell me who I am."

"I have told you many times, Boy."

"But tell me again, Grandfather.
 Tell me about my name."

"You know your name, Boy.
You know the story by heart."

"But it sounds better when you tell it.
Please tell it over and over, Grandfather.
I like to hear you say my name."

"Then listen carefully, Boy.
This may be the last time for telling the story.
The counting rope is almost filled with knots."

"This cannot be the last time, Grandfather.
Promise this will not be the last time."

"I cannot promise you anything, Boy.
I love you. I love you very much.
That is better than a promise."

"And I love you, Grandfather.
Tell me the story again. Please."

"Once there was a boy child...."

"That was I, wasn't it, Grandfather?"

"Yes, you were the boy child in the story."

"And I was very strong, wasn't I, Grandfather?"

"No, you were not strong, Boy.
   You were very little and very sick.
   We thought you were going to die."

"But *you* knew that I wouldn't die, Grandfather.
   Tell me that part again."

"One day when you were very sick
and your breath was too weak for crying,
two great blue horses came galloping by.
Suddenly they turned and looked at you.
You reached up your arms to them."

"And what did you say, Grandfather?"

"I said, 'See how the horses speak to him.
They are his brothers
from beyond the dark mountain.
This boy child will not die.
The blue horses have given him strength to live.' "

"And that is when you named me, isn't it?"

"Yes, we named you Boy Strength-of-Blue-Horses. It is a strong name."

"Did I need a strong name, Grandfather?"

"All children need strong names to grow strong."

"Did I grow strong, Grandfather?"

"Yes, Boy, you grew strong
  and you're becoming stronger every day.
  Some day you will be strong enough
  to cross over beyond the dark mountains."

"How strong must I be, Grandfather?
 Tell me that part again."

"You must be so strong, Boy,
 that you will not speak with anger
 even when your heart is filled with anger."

"And that is not all, Grandfather.
 Tell me the next part."

"You must be so strong, Boy,
 that you want to know
 what other people are thinking
 even when you are listening
 to your own thoughts."

"Now tell me the last part, Grandfather."

"You must be so strong, Boy,
  that you still stop to think
  of what happened yesterday
  and what will happen tomorrow
  in knowing what you want to do today."

"Is it hard to be strong like you, Grandfather?"

"Strong people are not born strong, Boy.
They become strong by thinking they are strong.
They dream of themselves as being strong enough
to cross over the dark mountains."

"Will I ever be strong enough to cross over
the dark mountains, Grandfather?"

"You already have crossed
some of the dark mountains, Boy.
The mountains have no beginning and no ending.
They are all around us.
We only know that we are crossing them
when we want to be weak
but choose to be strong."

"Maybe I will not be strong enough, Grandfather."

"Oh, yes, you will be, Boy Strength-of-Blue-Horses."

"Then you must keep telling me the story,
Grandfather.
You must never stop telling me the story."

"But I will stop telling the story, Boy,
when I have tied the last knot
on the counting rope.
Now that I have told the story again,
I tie another knot, just as I did before.
When the rope is filled with knots,
you will start telling the story to yourself.
That is the way you know you are strong.
That is the way you become strong."

Here's a Picture for Storytelling

by Kiyoaki Komoda

The Wonder of the Monarchs

by Harvey Gunderson,
pictures by Lee Ames

The Monarch caterpillar is born from a tiny egg. The caterpillar is only one tenth of an inch long when it is newly hatched, but it grows quickly. In three days it is about a half-inch long. In two weeks it is fullgrown.

A caterpillar sheds its skin four times during its growing period. During the two-week growing period it gains 3000 times its original weight and nearly 30 times its original length.

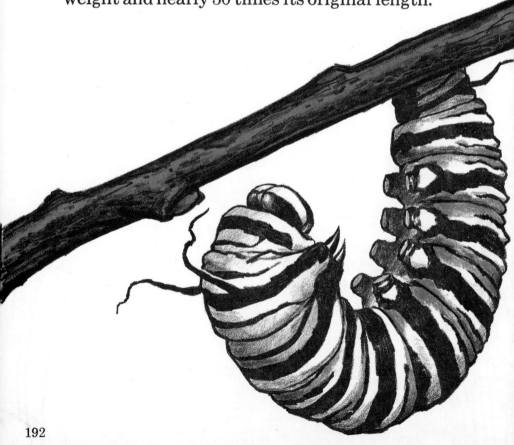

Then the caterpillar attaches itself to a twig to begin a miraculous change. It wriggles out of its old skin and its body becomes a bright green. This creature is no longer a caterpillar, but a chrysalis. Within the glossy green chrysalis the outline of a butterfly's body begins to appear.

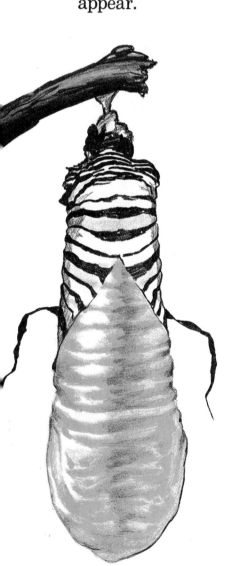
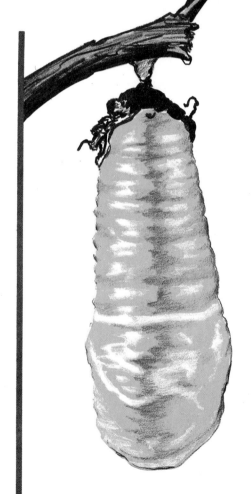

In about eight days the chrysalis changes color, from green to orange and black. The colors of the Monarch butterfly's wings are beginning to show through. All organs of the caterpillar's body have disappeared by now, and organs useful to the butterfly have formed.

At last it is the right moment! The transparent chrysalis cracks open, and the Monarch butterfly crawls out, head first.

The butterfly's wings are very small and its abdomen is very large. This is so because the abdomen is filled with a fluid that must be

pumped into the wings. As the wings become inflated, the abdomen gets smaller.

It takes several hours for the wings to dry, and another four or five hours for them to become strong.

From egg, to caterpillar, to chrysalis, to butterfly—three or four generations of Monarchs complete this cycle in a single summer. Then, sometime in September or October, the Monarchs begin to gather by the thousands for their great autumn migration. Each generation flies only a few hundred miles; then the females lay their eggs and die. It will be the third or fourth generation of Monarchs that reaches the south.

In the springtime, the Monarchs journey north. Once again, the females look for milkweed plants to scatter their tiny eggs on. And once again, the wonderful life cycle of the Monarch butterfly begins.

Here's a Picture for Storytelling

by Ted Schroeder

The Tiger,
The Brâhman,
and The Jackal

a folktale of India,
pictures by Mamoru Funai

Once upon a time a tiger was caught in
a trap. He tried in vain to get out through
the bars, and rolled and bit with rage and
grief when he failed.

By chance a poor Brâhman came by.

"Let me out of this cage, O pious one!" cried the tiger.

"Nay, my friend," replied the Brâhman mildly, "you would probably eat me if I did."

"Not at all!" swore the tiger with many oaths. "On the contrary, I would be forever grateful, and serve you as a slave!"

Now when the tiger sobbed and sighed and wept and swore, the pious Brâhman's heart softened, and at last he consented to open the door of the cage.

Out popped the tiger, and seizing the poor man, cried, "What a fool you are! What is to prevent my eating you now, for after being cooped up so long I am just terribly hungry!"

203

In vain the Brâhman pleaded for his life; the most he could gain was a promise to abide by the decision of the first three things he chose to question as to the justice of the tiger's action.

So the Brâhman first asked the *pipal* tree what it thought of the matter, but the *pipal* tree replied coldly, "What have you to complain about? Don't I give shade and shelter to every one who passes by, and don't they in turn tear down my branches to feed their cattle? Don't whimper—be a man!"

Then the Brâhman, sad at heart, went farther afield till he saw a buffalo turning a well-wheel; but he fared no better from it, for it answered, "You are a fool to expect gratitude! Look at me! While I gave milk they fed me on cotton-seed and oil-cake, but now I am dry, they yoke me here, and give me refuse as fodder!"

The Brâhman, still more sad, asked the road to give him its opinion.

"My dear sir," said the road, "how foolish you are to expect anything else! Here am I, useful to everybody, yet all, rich and poor, great and small, trample on me as they go past, giving me nothing but the ashes of their pipes, and the husks of their grains!"

On this the Brâhman turned back sorrowfully, and on the way he met a jackal, who called out, "Why, what's the matter, Mr. Brâhman? You look as miserable as a fish out of water!"

Then the Brâhman told him all that had occurred.

"How very confusing!" said the jackal, when the recital was ended. "Would you mind telling me all over again, for everything seems so mixed up!"

The Brâhman told it all over again, but the jackal shook his head in a distracted sort of way, and still could not understand.

"It's very odd," said he sadly, "but it all seems to go in at one ear and out at the other! I will go to the place where it all happened, and then perhaps I shall be able to give judgment."

So they returned to the cage, by which the tiger was waiting for the Brâhman, and sharpening his teeth and claws.

"You've been away a long time!" growled the savage beast. "But now let us begin our dinner."

"Our dinner!" thought the wretched Brâhman, as his knees knocked together with fright. "What a remarkably delicate way of putting it!"

"Give me five minutes, my lord!" he pleaded, "in order that I may explain matters to the jackal here, who is somewhat slow in his wits."

The tiger consented, and the Brâhman began the whole story over again, not missing a single detail, and spinning as long a yarn as possible.

"Oh, my poor brain! oh, my poor brain!" cried the jackal, wringing his paws. "Let me see! how did it all begin? You were in the cage, and the tiger came walking by—!"

"Pooh!" interrupted the tiger, "what a fool you are! *I* was in the cage."

"Of course!" cried the jackal, pretending to tremble with fright. "Yes, I was in the cage — no, I wasn't — dear! dear! where are my wits? Let me see — the tiger was in the Brâhman, and the cage came walking by — no, that's not it either! Well, don't mind me, but begin your dinner, for I shall never understand!"

"Yes, you shall!" returned the tiger, in a rage at the jackal's stupidity. "I'll make you understand! Look here—I am the tiger—"

"Yes, my lord!"

"And that is the Brâhman—"

"Yes, my lord!"

"And that is the cage—"

"Yes, my lord!"

"And I was in the cage—do you understand?"

"Yes,—no—Please, my lord—"

"Well?" cried the tiger, impatiently.

"Please, my lord!— how did you get in?"

"How!—why in the usual way, of course!"

"Oh dear me!—my head is beginning to whirl again! Please don't be angry, my lord, but what is the usual way?"

At this the tiger lost patience, and, jumping into the cage, cried, "This way! Now do you understand how it was?"

"Perfectly!" grinned the jackal, as he dexterously shut the door. "And if you will permit me to say so, I think matters will remain as they were!"

Keep a Poem in Your Pocket

Keep a poem in your pocket
and a picture in your head
and you'll never feel lonely
at night when you're in bed.

The little poem will sing to you
the little picture bring to you
a dozen dreams to dance to you
at night when you're in bed.

by Beatrice Schenk de Regniers,
picture by Kelly Oechsli